START-UP
GEOGRAPHY

PASSPORT TO THE WORLD

Anna Lee

Published by Evans Brothers Limited
2A Portman Mansions
Chiltern Street
London W1U 6NR

Reprinted 2005
Produced for Evans Brothers Limited by
White-Thomson Publishing Ltd.
2/3 St Andrew's Place
Lewes, East Sussex BN7 1UP

Printed in China by W K T Co. Ltd.

© Evans Brothers Limited 2003
Editor: Elaine Fuoco-Lang
Consultants: Lorraine Harrison, Senior Lecturer in
Geography Education at the University of Brighton
and Christine Bentall, Key Stage One teacher at
St Bartholomew's Church of England Primary
School, Brighton.
Designer: Tessa Barwick
Map artwork: The Map Studio

Cover: All photographs by WTPix

Lee, Anna
    Passport to the world. - (Start-up geography)
    1.Geography - Juvenile literature
    I.Title
    910

ISBN: 0 237 52477 5

Picture Acknowledgements:
All photographs by Alan Towse except WTPix (Chris
Fairclough) 5 *(right)*; WTPix 8 (Chris Fairclough) *(left)*;
Ecoscene/Stephen Coyne 8 *(right)*; WTPix 9 (Chris
Fairclough) *(left)*; WTPix (Dana Smillie) 9 *(top right)*;
WTPix 10 (Chris Fairclough) *(top)*; *Hodder Wayland
Picture Library* 10 *(bottom);* WTPix 20-21 (Chris
Fairclough) *(all)*.

Contents

Where we live

▶ **Here is a map of the United Kingdom.**

The key tells us what features are shown on the map.

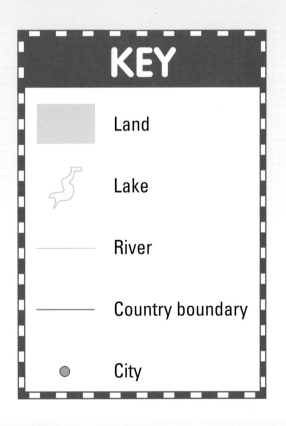

KEY

	Land
	Lake
	River
	Country boundary
●	City

SCOTLAND

Aberdeen

Edinburgh

NORTHERN IRELAND
Belfast

UNITED KINGDOM

River Shannon

Dublin

REPUBLIC OF IRELAND

WALES

River Severn

River Trent

Birmingham

ENGLAND

London

Cardiff

River Thames

0   100 miles

0   100 kilometres

Our school is in Birmingham, in England.
We know people all over the United Kingdom.

Jane's aunt lives in
Aberdeen, in Scotland.

Hanif's brother lives in
Cardiff, in Wales.

Can you find places you know on this map?

England   Scotland   Cardiff   Wales

▶ **Here is a map of the world.**

Can you find the United Kingdom?

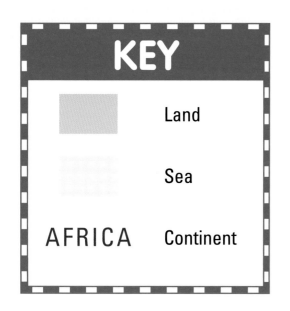

KEY

	Land
	Sea
AFRICA	Continent

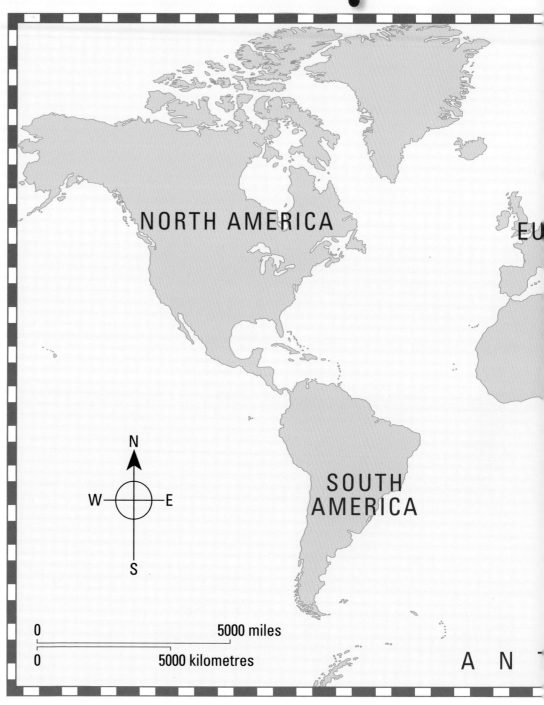

NORTH AMERICA

EU

SOUTH
AMERICA

N
W——E
S

0	5000 miles
0	5000 kilometres

A N T

the world

A S I A

CA

AUSTRALASIA

CTICA

There are seven continents in the world.

The United Kingdom is a country in the continent of Europe.

Which other countries can you name?

Can you find them on the map?

Different countries in the world

▶ **Sometimes people travel to different countries by plane.**

◀ **Paul has been to Greece on holiday. He sent back this postcard.**

travel Greece holiday postcard

▲ Hanif was born in Egypt.
His grandparents still live there.
They sent him this photograph.

Jane's mother sometimes visits
Indonesia for her work.

She brought back these chopsticks..

Do you have anything at home that
comes from another country?

Egypt Indonesia chopsticks

Packing for a holiday abroad

▶ **These people live in Australia.**

Australia has very hot summers.

◀ **These children live in Canada.**

In winter Canada is very cold.

Australia hot Canada cold

Which things would you take on a trip to Australia?

Which would you take to Canada in winter?

What things would you take to both?

Money and stamps in different countries

Many countries have their own **money**.

► Most countries in Europe use the **euro** and **cents**.

The United States uses **dollars** and cents.

Can you name the money we use in the United Kingdom?

money euro cents dollars

Different countries also have different stamps.

▼ **This letter is from Australia.**

It has an Australian stamp and postmark.

▼ **Here are some stamps from around the world.**

Where does our food come from?

The **food** we eat comes from all over the world.

The **labels** on this fruit tell us where the fruit was grown.

Which country is the orange from?
And the apple?

food labels

Here are some more foods that Paul and Marcus bought at the supermarket.

The brazil nuts are from Brazil.

The rice-crackers are from Japan.

The cheese is from Italy.

The rice is from Thailand.

Japan   Brazil   Italy   Thailand

Finding out about different places

▶ **Rosa's mum reads the newspapers to find out what is happening in different places in the world.**

◀ **You can find out what is happening in the world from watching television programmes, like this family in Greece.**

reads   newspapers   programmes

◀ Rosa likes to look on the internet to discover more about other countries in the world.

▶ Jacob's parents grew up in Jamaica. Marcus talks to them to find out about Jamaica.

internet Jamaica

A penfriend in South Africa

To find out more about life in South Africa, Jane wrote to a penfriend in Cape Town.

This is the letter her penfriend wrote back.

What does it tell us about South Africa?

Jane and her penfriend each kept a weather diary for a week.

96 Lagonda Crescent Grange Bay
Cape Town South Africa

Dear Jane

Thank you for your letter. It was interesting to hear about life in Birmingham. It must be fun to live in a flat with lots of other children nearby. I live on a farm and we have to drive a long way to visit friends.

It is nearly Christmas here and it is very hot. Christmas is in summer in South Africa. We are going to have a barbecue in our back garden on Christmas Day. After Christmas my family is going camping in a forest in the mountains. All sorts of birds and animals live in the forest. We might even see some monkeys! There is a big river and a waterfall, too. Where do you go on holiday in England?

I hope you are well.

Love from

Sally

Jane's chart (Birmingham)

	Monday	Tuesday	Wednesday	Thursday	Friday
hours	5	4	0	3	4
mm	1	2	1	1	0
temp	11	10	11	9	11

Sally's chart (Cape Town)

	Monday	Tuesday	Wednesday	Thursday	Friday
hours	7	8	8	6	5
mm	0	0	0	0	1
temp	26	30	32	31	30

Was Birmingham or Cape Town sunnier for that week?

weather diary ... **19**

Our world

Here is another map of the world, with some pictures of different places in the world.

Which places on the map do you know?

What do you know about them?

How could you find out more?

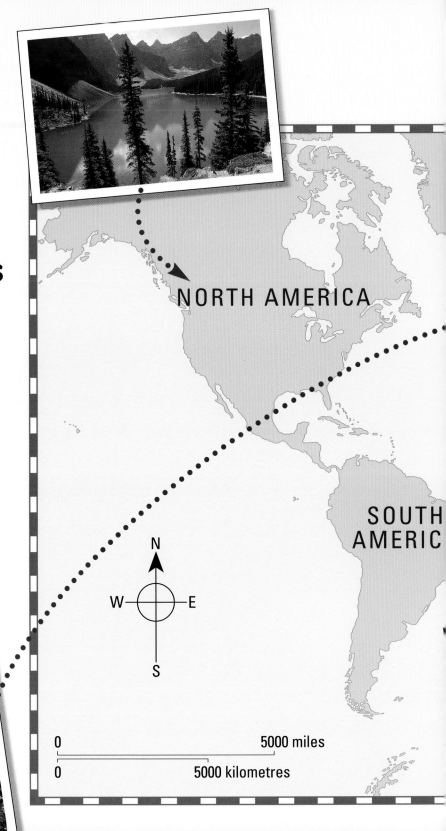

NORTH AMERICA

SOUTH AMERIC

N
W — E
S

| 0 | 5000 miles |
| 0 | 5000 kilometres |

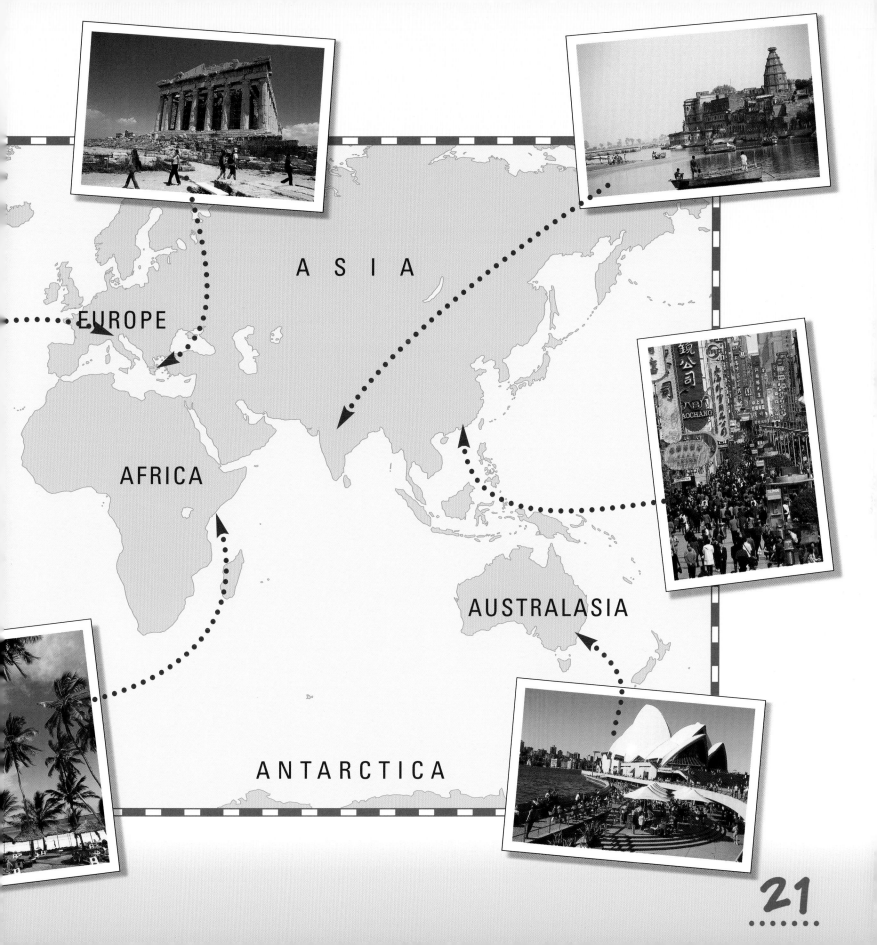

EUROPE

ASIA

AFRICA

AUSTRALASIA

ANTARCTICA

21

Further information for

New words listed in the text:

Australia	countries	Greece	key	reads	weather diary
Brazil	country	holiday	labels	Scotland	world
Canada	dollars	hot	map	South Africa	
Cape Town	Egypt	Indonesia	money	stamps	
Cardiff	England	internet	newspapers	Thailand	
cents	euro	Italy	penfriend	travel	
chopsticks	Europe	Jamaica	postcard	trip	
cold	features	Japan	postmark	United Kingdom	
continents	food	Kenya	programmes	Wales	

Possible Activities

SPREAD ONE

On a map of the British Isles mark on the places where children's parents/friends/family live.

Make a chart showing whose relatives live close by and whose live the furthest away.

Look in a national newspaper and mark on a map of the British Isles all the places that are mentioned.

SPREAD TWO

On a map of the world show where children have been on their holidays.

Conduct a survey on holiday destinations and make a graph to show which destination is the most popular.

SPREAD THREE

Choose a foreign country and investigate which foods are eaten there, what clothes are worn, and what the weather is like.

Ask the children to describe how they would travel to the chosen country.

SPREAD FOUR

Discuss what the children take with them on holiday.

Ask the children to bring in photographs of their holiday.

SPREAD FIVE

Design a stamp(s) for a special occasion for the school, town or country.

Parents and Teachers

SPREAD SIX

Discuss which foods are common to certain countries, for example, pasta - Italy, curry - India, fajitas/nachos - Mexico.

Collect and taste different foods from around the world. Make a graph to show which food was liked the most and which food was liked the least.

If the foods are in containers or packets attach the empty packets to a map of the world to show where they are from.

SPREAD SEVEN

Invite someone to talk about what it is like to live in a foreign country.

Watch the news and write down different countries that are in the news. Why are these countries mentioned?

Research a chosen country on the internet looking at more specific points such as what the houses are like and what animals and plants are common to the chosen country.

SPREAD EIGHT

Ask the children if they have penfriends in other countries. Mark on a map of the world where the penfriends live.

Make your own basic weather chart for the week saying if it was sunny, cloudy, rainy or windy.

SPREAD NINE

Ask the children to bring in postcards they have received and put them onto a map of the world.

Further Information

BOOKS

FOR CHILDREN

Around the World: Clothes by Godfrey Hall (Hodder Wayland 2000)

Around the World: Food by Godfrey Hall (Hodder Wayland 2000)

Around the World: Houses by Godfrey Hall (Hodder Wayland 2000)

Where We Live by Sally Hewitt (Franklin Watts 2000)

FOR ADULTS

Handbook of Primary Geography by Roger Carter (Ed) (The Geographical Association 1998)

WEBSITES

http://www.standards.dfee.gov.uk/schemes/geography

http://www.learn.co.uk

http://www.schoolzone.co.uk

Index